Anxiety

A Practical And Specialized Guide To Emotional Control And Management

(How To Overcome Anxiety By Developing Into A Peace Warrior)

Kyriakos Chatzakis

TABLE OF CONTENT

Introduction 1

Chapter 1: Baby Steps Towards Your Objectives And Wants 17

Chapter 2: Maintaining Your Brain Health 33

Chapter 3: How Should I Manage Anticipatory Anxiety? 46

Chapter 4: Be Alert Regarding Your Thoughts 65

Chapter 5: Normal View And Magnified View. 79

Chapter 7: The Range Of Professional Recommendations 88

Chapter 9: Taking Control Of Stress And Anxiety 108

Chapter 10: What Is Stress? 110

Chapter 11: The Distinction Between Anxiety And Tension 113

Chapter 12: Trying To Act Happy 116

Chapter 13: Emotional Mastery In Interpersonal Relationships: Enhancing Communication And Bonding 128

Chapter 14: Causes Of Bipolar Disorder And Anxiety Disorders 133

Chapter 15: How To You Stress Free 145

Chapter 16: Anxiety Disorder 159

Introduction

According to a study conducted by the National Institute of Mental Health, anxiety disorders are more prevalent among American women than among men, whereas alcohol and drug abuse are the most prevalent forms of mental illness among American men. Anxiety disorders affect approximately 17% of the U.S. population, or approximately fifty million individuals. These individuals may have experienced anxiety disorders such as phobias or panic attacks in the past year. Approximately one-fourth of adults may suffer from anxiety disorders at some point in their lives, and these conditions can take many forms. Sadly, only a small fraction of those in need actually receive treatment. In the past two decades, anxiety and panic attacks have reached epidemic proportions, and the subject has received extensive media coverage. As the first decade of the twenty-first century draws to a close, new concerns regarding economic instability, the rapid degradation of the environment, and global terrorism have contributed to a growing trend of communal anxiety. Multiple factors have contributed to the emergence of these new unknowns.

Why do so many people suffer from anxiety, phobias, and panic attacks? According to what I've read, anxiety disorders result from an accumulation of stress over time. Stress, especially chronic stress, is a significant contributor to the development of anxiety disorders such as panic attacks, phobias, and obsessive-compulsive disorders, although other factors undoubtedly play a role. Despite the fact that we all bear some degree of responsibility for the stress in our lives, our upbringing also plays a significant role. The rising prevalence of anxiety disorders can be partially explained by the fact that the average Westerner is under more stress than ever before in history. It could be argued that people have always dealt with stressful social events such as wars, famines, epidemics, and economic depressions; however, there are at least two reasons to believe that the current level of stress is greater than it has ever been. Our environment and the social order we maintain have undergone more profound changes in the last thirty years than in the previous three hundred. In a very brief period of time, digital information technology has brought about significant changes in our way of life. Due to the rapid acceleration of modern life and technological development, people no longer have sufficient time to adapt to these changes. In addition, there are a growing number of uncertainties regarding our individual futures. Since late 2008, people all over the world have been experiencing the effects of the worst economic crisis since the Great Depression, and as this book prepares for publication in late 2010, many questions remain unanswered. Many scientists believe we have already passed a critical threshold in terms of global warming, extreme weather, biodiversity loss, and the destruction of natural ecosystems, placing the future of global ecology in grave peril. Once these inflection points are passed, it will be difficult to return to the world as we know it. As a result of nuclear proliferation, the terrifying possibility has emerged that terrorist organisations may develop nuclear weapons and use them against developed nations. Such conditions create a social climate that is conducive to anxiety, and the list of unknowns could be endless. When a society as a whole is more anxious and uncertain, anxiety disorders tend to become more prevalent. Here's an instance:

In conclusion, cultural values are a mystery. We need a community-wide set of values that is consistent and authoritative (traditionally prescribed by society and religion). People become helpless as a result of being left to fend for themselves. uthoritative set of values acknowledged by the greater community (traditionally prescribed by society and religion). People become helpless as a result of being left to fend for themselves. Individuals must possess the ability to construct their own meaning and moral order in a society where media constantly bombards consumers with competing worldviews and norms.

Many people in today's modern society have difficulty achieving a sense of stability or consistency in their lives as a result of the cumulative effect of all these factors. One of the negative effects of stress that is exacerbated by a lack of coping mechanisms is the development of anxiety disorders. Additional outcomes include substance use disorders, depression, and an increase in the incidence of degenerative diseases.

In the past two decades, there has been a plethora of excellent literature on anxiety disorders. The majority of these renowned works are written in a descriptive style. The vast majority of these works have focused on providing readers with a fundamental understanding of anxiety disorders, as opposed to discussing therapy techniques or providing actual recovery strategies.

I set out to write this guide for two primary reasons: I to help others recognise what skills they lacked, and (ii) to provide detailed, actionable instructions and guided practice to help them acquire those skills and overcome their anxiety, phobias, and panic attacks.

This guide contains a substantial amount of background information, but its primary focus is on the development of coping skills and the identification of recovery-promoting activities. These characteristics identify the present document as a workbook.

This book probably contains little new information. The books listed at the end of each chapter provide additional information on the topics covered in that section, including, but not limited to, stress reduction, physical activity, coping with panic attacks, exposure therapy, feeling and labelling emotions, speaking up for yourself, improving your diet and lifestyle, and enhancing your sense of well-being through meditation. In these chapters, a summary of the material presented in those books is provided. My goal was to write a book outlining all the necessary strategies for coping with anxiety issues and to make it available to as many people as possible. The more you can incorporate these strategies into your own treatment plan, the quicker and more effectively you will recover. This workbook takes a strongly holistic approach. It discusses interventions that will affect your life on multiple levels, including your body, behaviour, emotions, mind, interpersonal relationships, self-esteem, and spirituality. Prior popular approaches to panic and phobias have primarily emphasised behavioural and cognitive (or mental) techniques. These remain the foundation of any successful program for the treatment of all anxiety disorders and are of utmost importance. These methods are covered in four chapters of this manual. Chapter 6 provides essential concepts and coping strategies for learning to manage panic attacks. Exposure is an essential component of any program for overcoming agoraphobia, social phobia, or other specific phobias, as described in Chapter 7. The eighth and ninth chapters present strategies for learning to counter unhelpful "self-talk" and erroneous beliefs that tend to perpetuate daily anxiety. Additionally, relaxation and personal health are of paramount importance. As previously stated, anxiety disorders are caused by chronic, accumulative stress. The fact that the majority of people with anxiety disorders tend to be in a chronic state of physiological hyperarousal is evidence of this stress. Recovery depends on adopting lifestyle changes that promote a more relaxed, balanced, and healthy outlook on life; in other words, changes that enhance your physical health. The strategies and skills presented in the chapters on relaxation, exercise, and nutrition serve as a necessary foundation for the remaining skills presented in this manual. Exposure, for instance, is much easier to implement if you have first learned how to induce a deep state of relaxation. When you are physically healthy and relaxed, you will also find it easier to identify and alter negative internal dialogue.

In the same way that learning positive self-talk habits will help you feel better, improving your physical health through proper relaxation, exercise, and nutrition will decrease your propensity for negative attitudes and self-talk.

When you feel good, you will also think well.

On the opposite end of the spectrum, a lack of direction or personal meaning in life can increase the risk of developing anxiety disorders. Panic attacks and agoraphobia, particularly when they involve a fear of being confined or unable to escape, may represent a feeling of "being stuck" or "having nowhere to go" in life. Given the complexity of modern society and the absence of an externally prescribed set of values, it is common to feel confused and uncertain about your life's meaning and direction. By increasing your connection to a larger sense of purpose and, as appropriate, cultivating your own spirituality, you can develop a sense of meaning that will aid in alleviating your anxiety. This is an important consideration when treating anxiety disorders and likely the majority of other behaviour disorders as well (see Chapter 20). In conclusion, for a comprehensive and lasting solution to anxiety disorders, a model that integrates all of the approaches presented in this book is required. Recovery from anxiety requires interventions on all levels of the individual. A final significant point merits mention. For you to successfully utilise the skills presented in this workbook, you will need a strong commitment and consistent motivation. It is possible to achieve long-term recovery on your own if you are self-motivated and disciplined. However, going it alone is not always the best or most effective option. Many readers will choose to use this workbook in conjunction with consulting a therapist who specialises in the treatment of anxiety disorders. A therapist can provide structure and support, as well as help you tailor the concepts and strategies in this workbook to your unique circumstances. Some of you may also find support groups and treatment groups (particularly for agoraphobia and social phobia) to be extremely beneficial. A support group structure can motivate and sustain your interest in acquiring the necessary recovery skills. Numerous individuals appear to benefit from the motivation, structure, and support that a group can offer. You must ultimately choose the best course of action for yourself. If you decide to seek outside assistance for your problem, you should contact a specialist in the treatment of anxiety disorders for assistance in determining the optimal treatment format. The Anxiety Disorders Association of America provides a directory of such specialists in the United States and Canada (ADAA). Enter your city or zip code on their website, sadaa.org, and click on "Search" (see Appendix 1 for further information). The ADAA also provides a state-by-state directory of support groups for anxiety disorders.

Using the strategies and exercises presented in this workbook, it is entirely possible to overcome your problem with panic, phobias, or anxiety by yourself. However, it is equally valuable and appropriate to use this book as a supplement to working with a therapist or group therapy programme, if you so choose. Regardless of the approach you choose, there is a great deal of assistance available. When you commit to and consistently implement the approach outlined in this book, you can alleviate or eliminate your anxiety problems.

Chapter 1: Baby Steps Towards Your Objectives And Wants

When we are slacking, when it's difficult to even get up and get started with the day. When we feel desperate to escape a situation but lack the motivation to take action. When we choose to take the easy way out by complaining or blaming others instead of taking responsibility (and let's face it, we've all done this), the best we can do is put ourselves in a routine, in time slots. Remember your school days? We used to have eight periods, excluding recess, and study five or more subjects daily in those few hours, but how productive were we when we returned home from school? Were we capable of producing the same amount? Most likely not!

What about your office work when the world shifted to digital? Could you work from home for a specific period of time without interruption or distraction? Could you set a cutoff time of 7 or 8 p.m., or whatever time you used to work in the office? No? Why?

Due to the ever-decreasing attention span of humans (it is said to have decreased from 12 seconds in 2000 to about 8 seconds now), it is becoming increasingly difficult to perform focused work without a setup. We must put ourselves in a routine to best utilise our time and extract the most from us. We need to discipline ourselves and be consistent.

"You will never change your life until you alter a daily habit. The key to your success lies in your daily habits." - John C. Maxwell

It is acceptable to begin modestly or even to fail; do not be too hard on yourself. Nobody can run a marathon on the very first day, but what's important is to show up and be willing to grow every single day. If on the first day you schedule only 15 to 20 minutes for physical activity, that's fine; we don't have to begin with an hour. If needed, keep good enough gaps in between, don't burden yourself.

E.g.: \s• Work for 20-25 mins (one session), take a break for 5 mins and work again for another 20-25 mins, followed by another break of 15 mins, and repeat it for the next hour.

- Set aside a separate occasion to reward yourself. Take a tea break, have a conversation, or watch an episode on Netflix, or reward yourself in any way you choose.

Again, plan for the next one to two hours of work.

Initially, you are not required to schedule or time slot your entire day. Do so for no more than four to five hours per day, but once you've established a routine, stick to it, show up, and gradually increase your time and endurance.

Pause if you are having difficulty completing a task due to distractions. First, determine the type of distraction you are experiencing. Are these distractions physical, such as background noise, or mental, such as intrusive thoughts?

If they are physical distractions, they are simple to eliminate once identified. Next time you begin working, you should address these issues first. However, if it is a mental distraction, take a five-minute break, acknowledge the thoughts, and allow them to pass. Let everything pass you by as you observe them as if you were watching a movie. Do not attempt to become involved. Take yourself out of the equation and simply observe. Observe your mind having multiple thoughts. It would not last long, so you should return to your work. Consider spending no more than 5-10 minutes on it.

You can also use techniques such as Pomodoro to concentrate on tasks. It is estimated that the average mind wanders between 15 and 20 percent of the time *12, whereas focus activities such as Pomodoro allow you to focus 100 percent on a task for 25 minutes straight. Focus is crucial. It is acceptable to work 1-2 hours less than usual, but you must do so with complete concentration. Engage in the work. Get into the zone, whatever you're doing.

2) FIND A PARTNER FOR ACCOUNTABILITY: It is always easier to complete tasks with others. It is much easier to trek with a group than on your own. Consequently, you should have someone with whom you can share your routine, schedule, and do much of it

together, pushing each other through phases of reluctance and resistance.

- Motivate one another to complete the tasks, and find someone who has also struggled to get started. Or someone who would readily assist you in regaining your footing.

If you do not have anyone to collaborate with, enrol in classes and begin your activities with a group. Whether it be a yoga, Zumba, or pottery class, or an online meditation or writers club. To increase accountability, enrol in classes and pay for the sessions/seminars on your own. Find people and participate in activities with and around them.

Remember how it was easier to complete a math problem or an art project when the entire class was working on it? Working in a group makes it easier to complete an entire HIIT or yoga session than working alone. It is easier to run a marathon with friends than on your own. Compared to solo workouts, group workouts not only help you be more consistent, but also improve your mental, physical, and emotional health by a significant amount. Additionally, group activities reduce stress levels by a whopping 26% *13).

Even better in the age of digitalization is to choose an offline class. Maintain a human connection! Have you ever had days when you did not feel like leaving the house, but once you sat down with your friends, you realised you could not have imagined a better way to spend the day? Meet and interact with people.

Most importantly, select your personnel. The more healthy your social circle, the healthier you will be!

3) EXERCISE!!! Work up a sweat. Go for a run! Wherever the road takes you, run ceaselessly as if there were no endpoint. Plan the Himalayan trek you've always desired to undertake. Start slowly, but get started. Whatever is present in your mind and body, you must expel it.

Do you know how canines relieve stress and other forms of emotional tension? They disperse! They restore their energy balance by shaking. And physical activity, preferably an outdoor activity such as running, biking, hiking, swimming, or surfing, will do the same for you. Consume yourself and absorb nature.

Try this for a month without breaks or cheat days, and you will notice the difference.

Exercise not only improves physical health, but also mental and emotional health. In addition to reducing anxiety, depression, and social withdrawal, it enhances self-esteem and cognitive function. *14 WHO claims, 'People who are insufficiently active have a 20% to 30% increased risk of death compared to people who are sufficiently active' *21

4) MEDITATE: Devote some time each day to meditation. Give your mind the necessary break! Start with 10 minutes per day and increase gradually. Start at a convenient time and transition to a fixed schedule later. But get started! Mediation has numerous benefits, including enhancement of cognitive

abilities, reduction of physical pain, and improvement of mental and emotional health. *20

5) START EARLY: Try to rise with the sun and witness the world before the sun rises. I, too, am not a morning person, but you should make the effort to adhere to that 5 AM schedule. If you have always desired to experience it but have found it difficult to do so, the following advice may be of assistance:

Do not set multiple alarms; instead, have just one and prepare your mind to be alert to recognise it the moment it rings (when we know there are multiple alarms, we don't give any of them enough importance; we value scarce things more than abundant ones). Place the phone/alarm clock in an inconvenient location so that you must get out of bed to turn it off.

Include a favourite activity in your morning routine to encourage you not to skip it.

Have a partner who will motivate you to get out of bed when you procrastinate, and do the same for them.

- Sounds amateurish, doesn't it, to whisper to your pillow what time you want to wake up the following morning? But give it a shot. It does work! It aids in the wiring of the brain; when you tell your pillow to wake you up, you are actually telling your mind to do so.

Rewiring the brain so that you no longer require extra hours of sleep in order to attain your goals and desires. Utilizing the existing belief system (you must work hard or sacrifice 'aaram' (rest) in order to reap rewards) to our advantage.

6) CELEBRATE SMALL VICTORIES: Whether it's waking up at the desired time, completing a scheduled task, going for an exhilarating run, completing a project, or anything that makes you feel even the tiniest bit proud of yourself, you should celebrate these victories. Every small victory merits celebration!

7) RETAIN CONSISTENCY: Last but not least, the most important advice, which we all know but have difficulty implementing. Show up each and every day! Unless you are consistent, the results of your actions will be minimal.

"Greatness is not always necessary for success. It involves consistency. Consistent effort yields success.

"Greatness will arrive" – Dwayne "The Rock" Johnson

What I do daily matters more than what I do occasionally. – Gretchen Rubin

No one but ourselves is the obstacle we must overcome. It is the fundamental cause of all procrastination. A mind without training is like a horse without a jockey. Develop your mind! Take responsibility for your actions and life.

A quick sum up:

Consider the following baby steps to begin moving toward your objectives:

1) Establish a routine and schedule your day according to your preferred activities and the amount of time you wish to devote to each. This would aid you in avoiding procrastination and

time-wasting on activities such as social media, OTT platforms, etc.

2) To have an accountability partner with whom to complete daily tasks. To participate in group activities through participation in sessions and classes. It has been demonstrated that group activities have a positive effect on mental and emotional health.

3) Exercise! Not only will it improve your physical health, but also your mental and emotional well-being.

4) Commence the day early! 5 a.m. has a unique allure that can only be discovered through personal experience.

5) Rejoice in small victories. Only a collection of small victories will lead you to that large victory.

6) Be consistent! Taking small steps on a daily basis is always more productive than taking one large step occasionally.

Chapter 2: Maintaining Your Brain Health

Maintaining a healthy brain is essential for a healthy, happy, and productive life. Your brain controls every aspect of your life, and if it's not operating properly, it can lead to serious problems such as depression, anxiety, and even physical illness. Maintaining a healthy brain is essential for maintaining mental clarity and focus, reducing stress, and enhancing memory and concentration.

Sleep Hygiene

Sleep hygiene refers to the habits and environmental factors that can affect our ability to sleep well. It consists of both physical and mental activities that should be performed to ensure quality sleep.

Mental activities include: Creating a calming environment for sleep: It may be easier to fall asleep and stay asleep if the bedroom is kept dark, quiet, and at a comfortable temperature.

Establishing a pre-sleep routine: Activities like taking a warm bath, reading a book, or meditating can help to relax the body and mind, making it easier to fall asleep.

Stress can disrupt sleep, making it difficult to fall asleep and remain asleep. Taking steps to reduce stress can improve the quality of sleep.

The blue light emitted by electronic devices can disrupt sleep, making it difficult to fall asleep and remain asleep.

Limiting electronic device use prior to bedtime can improve sleep quality.

By adhering to these recommendations for good sleep hygiene, we can improve the quality of our sleep and awaken feeling more rested and energised.

Sleep is an essential component of our overall health and well-being, and improving our sleep hygiene can help us feel our best.

Getting Adequate Sleep

A person's mental and physical health can be significantly impacted by their sleep quantity and quality. To feel refreshed and alert, most adults require between 7 and 9 hours of sleep per night.

The quality of sleep is equally as important as the quantity, so to ensure a healthy night's rest, create a comfortable, distraction-free environment. This Web Page | 29

entails keeping a bedroom cool, dark, and quiet. In addition to avoiding caffeine, alcohol, and heavy meals late at night, screen time should be limited before bed. Developing a regular sleep schedule may also aid in enhancing sleep quality.

Getting sufficient, high-quality sleep each night can improve mood and concentration, increase energy levels, improve physical health, and protect against mental health issues such as anxiety and depression.

The total amount of time spent sleeping over a 24-hour period is the sleep duration. Depending on age, lifestyle, and other factors, the average adult requires between 7 and 9 hours of sleep each night. Teenagers and young adults, for instance, require more sleep than adults, and athletes may require additional sleep to recover from strenuous activities.

Medications and medical conditions, such as sleep apnea, can also affect the duration of sleep. Insufficient sleep can cause a variety of symptoms, including fatigue, irritability, and concentration difficulties.

Quality Time: The quality of rest experienced during sleep is referred to as the quality of sleep. Deep, restorative sleep that is uninterrupted and allows the body to enter a state of relaxation characterise quality sleep. The quality of sleep can be affected by stress, medications, and lifestyle choices.

Obtaining the appropriate quantity and quality of sleep is crucial for maintaining a healthy brain. Sleep allows the brain to process and store information by recharging it. In addition, it helps regulate mood and energy levels, as well as appetite.

bolster the immune system Moreover, quality sleep has been associated with enhanced cognitive performance and enhanced decision-making abilities.

Stress, lifestyle habits, and medications can all affect sleep quality, so it is important to take steps to ensure that you get the best quality of sleep possible each night.

Cognitive Treatment

Cognitive therapy is a form of psychotherapy that focuses on altering a person's thoughts, emotions, and behaviours. It is based on the premise that our thoughts, emotions, and behaviours are interconnected and mutually influential.

Cognitive therapy is used to treat numerous mental health conditions, including depression, anxiety, eating disorders, and addiction.

Cognitive therapy focuses on assisting individuals in modifying negative thought patterns and behaviours that inhibit optimal functioning. It is based on the premise that our thoughts, emotions, and behaviours are interconnected and mutually influential. Cognitive therapy assists individuals in recognising and challenging their irrational and negative thought patterns, which can lead to more positive and realistic thought patterns. It also emphasises the significance of acquiring new skills and coping mechanisms for managing stress, anxiety, and depression.

By focusing on the present rather than dwelling on the past, it can help people learn how to better manage their emotions and behaviour. In addition, it encourages individuals to become more conscious of their thoughts and emotions and how they influence their actions and reactions. By recognising negative and irrational thought patterns, individuals can learn how to replace them with healthier and more productive alternatives.

CT can be an effective method for maintaining brain health by teaching individuals how to better manage their thoughts, emotions, and behaviours. It can assist individuals in confronting their fears and anxieties and working through difficult emotions.

Cognitive therapy can also help individuals develop the skills necessary to manage stress, anxiety, and depression, as well as to overcome addiction.

People can learn to recognise and challenge irrational thoughts, manage their emotions and behaviour, and develop the skills necessary to live a healthy and happy life through the use of cognitive therapy (CT). CT is an effective tool for maintaining mental health and well-being, and it can be a great way to maintain optimal brain health and function.

Overall, cognitive therapy can be an effective method for preserving mental health. Cognitive therapy can help you develop healthier patterns of thinking and behaviour, which can lead to improved mental health, by identifying and challenging negative thoughts and beliefs, learning new skills for stress management, and addressing underlying issues.

Medication, Supplements, Fruits, and Foods That Maintain a Healthy Brain

Medications and nutritional supplements can play a significant role in maintaining brain health. They can prevent or mitigate cognitive decline, mood disorders, anxiety, and other neurological conditions associated with ageing.

Various mental health conditions, including depression and anxiety, can be treated with medication. Antidepressants and other psychotropic drugs can reduce the symptoms of mental illness and enhance mental health overall.

health. Additionally, certain medications can improve concentration, memory, and other cognitive functions.

Brain health can also be supported by dietary supplements. Omega-3 fatty acids, ginkgo Biloba, and other antioxidants can aid in brain protection and cognitive enhancement. Vitamins of the B-complex and other micronutrients can support cognitive health.

In addition to medication and supplements, alterations to one's lifestyle can promote brain health. Regular physical exercise and activity can enhance mental clarity and concentration. Yoga, meditation, and deep breathing are anxiety-relieving and well-being-enhancing stress management techniques. Eating a well-balanced diet, obtaining sufficient rest, and engaging in social activities can also contribute to brain health.

In general, medication and supplements can aid in the improvement and maintenance of cognitive health. They should be used in conjunction with lifestyle modifications for optimal results. Before beginning any new medication or supplement, it is essential to consult with your doctor to ensure that it is safe and appropriate for your unique situation.

It is essential to keep in mind that medication and supplements are not a replacement for proper medical care. Regular checkups, mental health screenings, and other preventive measures are essential for preserving health and wellbeing.

Chapter 3: How Should I Manage Anticipatory Anxiety?

Anxiety can manifest in numerous forms. It could resemble anxiety regarding a trip to the doctor, a meeting with a new supervisor, or even a potential natural disaster.

In the absence of details, anticipatory anxiety is the intense fear that a future event may go awry or become uncontrollable.

It is normal to experience some anxiety regarding the future. The majority of individuals make assumptions about what may or may not occur in their lives.

However, it may indicate anticipatory anxiety if you worry about potential negative outcomes, especially prior to an event or unpleasant situation.

What is impending anxiety?

According to anxiety therapist Heather Forward of Lawrenceville, Georgia, anticipatory anxiety is anxiety worry. It occurs because our minds are preoccupied with potential future negative outcomes of the anxiety-producing trigger.

There may be situational to recurring anxiety.

Situational anticipatory anxiety may be present if you are concerned about how your first day of work or school will go, or if you consider the myriad ways your first date could go horribly wrong.

According to certified psychotherapist Carley Trillow of Cleveland, Ohio, situational anxiety typically disappears once the triggering event has passed. "For example, a person may experience anxiety in the week preceding performance evaluations. The evaluation's conclusion will alleviate situational tension.

As a trained psychiatrist in Houston, Nereida Gonzalez-Berrios explains, "If you frequently feel anxious for days, weeks, or even months prior to an anxiety-provoking event, it may be a persistent issue."

In addition, Gonzalez-Berrios clarifies that anticipatory anxiety is not a disorder by itself. It is a genuine generalised anxiety disorder, not a panic disorder (GAD).

Variations of anticipative anxiety

According to Gonzalez-Berrios, anticipatory anxiety may stem from the fear of undertaking a new, unknown task or of failing.

Additionally, it may be caused by underlying mental health issues such as:

• GAD. This syndrome is characterised by excessive, unwarranted tension and anxiety. It frequently involves multiple stressors and may affect your interpersonal and professional relationships. Since at least six months ago, these unwarranted concerns have almost daily occurrences.

• phobias specific to certain situations. This condition, which is commonly referred to as "basic phobias," is characterised by an intense fear of a specific situation or object. Real, palpable danger is frequently outweighed by dread. Fears of heights, animals, flying, and injections are examples of common phobias.

- Disorder of social anxiety. This syndrome results in an intense aversion to social situations. This anxiety disorder, also known as social phobia, is characterised by an intense fear of other people's criticism, making it distressing or unpleasant to perform or speak in front of an audience.

Additionally, those with obsessive-compulsive disorder experience anticipation anxiety, according to Gonzalez-Berrios (OCD). This is especially true when an individual with

OCD fears that their obsessive rituals will prevent them from engaging in social or professional activities.

Manifestations of anticipatory anxiety

Since anticipatory anxiety is not a recognised mental health condition, it may be difficult to determine if you have it. You would typically exhibit signs of general anxiety, but the trigger would be different (something that has not yet occurred).

With anticipatory anxiety, a sudden surge of unease or even an overwhelming sense of dread may be experienced.

According to Forward, anticipatory anxiety shares many similarities with GAD, also known as "normal" anxiety.

According to the National Institute of Mental Health, 5.7% of American adults will experience GAD at some point in their lives.

After exhibiting symptoms almost daily for six months in accordance with the Diagnostic and Statistical Manual of Mental Disorders, Fifth Edition (DSM-5), you would be diagnosed with GAD.

At this time, a mental health professional would specifically be on the lookout for three or more of the following six symptoms:

• feeling nervous, restless, or tense

- having trouble concentrating or feeling as if your mind is "blank"

- becoming agitated • being easily exhausted • having tense muscles • experiencing sleep difficulties, such as difficulty falling or staying asleep or restless, uncomfortable sleep

If you recognise any of these symptoms and they are frequently triggered by the anticipation of potential future events, you may be suffering from anticipatory anxiety.

Additional indicators of impending anxiety

It's likely that you're experiencing anticipatory anxiety if you find yourself focusing intensely on feared, undesirable outcomes, especially if you notice an increase in feelings of frustration and helplessness as a result.

According to Gonzalez-Berrios, the subsequent are additional signs of anticipatory anxiety:

• experiencing ongoing apprehension or trepidation about an upcoming event • constantly anticipating failure • being prone to distraction • experiencing trepidation • thinking irrationally for no apparent reason • having trouble remaining seated after excessively worrying

Involvement of anticipatory anxiety in panic disorder

Anticipatory anxiety is a prominent sign of panic disorder, which frequently causes panic attacks.

An additional symptom of panic disorder is anxiety or tension regarding a potential panic attack. In other words, you anticipate having a panic attack and are therefore extremely anxious.

Agoraphobia is another disorder associated with panic disorder and anticipatory anxiety.

The fear of public places is a common symptom of agoraphobia. A person with agoraphobia has difficulty leaving their home due to their fear of these frequently crowded places.

In other words, you attempt to avoid leaving your home out of fear of potential danger.

Cognitive distortions and anticipatory anxiety: Is there a relationship?

Cognitive distortions occur when "your ideas are distorted; what you are thinking and what you are telling yourself are not entirely accurate," according to therapist Angela Ficken of Boston, Massachusetts.

Ficken adds that because anxiety distorts thoughts, they are frequently distorted when one is anxious. It cautions us to be cautious, which, while sometimes useful (don't go down that dark alley; there may be danger), does not always provide the full picture.

According to Forward, the following cognitive errors or thought processes can contribute to anticipatory anxiety:

- Tarot card interpretation (trying to predict the future)

- mental acuity (trying to guess what others are thinking or feeling)

- Should-haves and might-haves (ruminating on different outcomes)

- apocalyptic belief (exaggerating situations by assuming the worst will happen)

- magnifying glass (exaggerating situations by making small issues large)

- Thinking that is black-and-white or polarised (assuming something is extremely good or extremely bad)

Five recommendations for alleviating anticipation anxiety

This advice may help you manage anticipatory anxiety regardless of your mental health.

1. Get sufficient rest

When you are tense and anxious, it can be difficult to fall asleep. You could feel more anxious if you don't get enough sleep.

Finding techniques to sleep through the night is crucial, especially given that sleep deprivation can exacerbate the symptoms of anticipatory anxiety.

If you control your coffee consumption, begin a meditation practise, and use nighttime relaxation techniques, you may find it easier to establish a sleep routine that is beneficial to your health.

2. Get active

Exercise is the key to reducing anticipatory anxiety. It may help reduce anxiety and stress symptoms.

Even 15 to 30 minutes of daily physical activity, according to Trillow, may have a positive effect. You may do this by dancing, walking, or practising yoga, among other activities. When anxiety levels are high, the body loses the ability to regulate itself. Movement facilitates this.

3. Practice being present

According to Forward, engaging in calming activities such as diaphragmatic breathing, rhythmic breathing, meditation, colouring, or sketching may be quite advantageous.

She asserts that mindfulness is a valuable skill that aims to keep you in the present, preventing you from dwelling on the future, which is the defining feature of anticipatory anxiety.

4. Shift your attention

There are simple measures you can take to divert your attention from the stressful situation.

Ficken recommends scheduling an enjoyable activity shortly after the anticipated event.

If you are anxious about an upcoming presentation, Ficken suggests "treating yourself to something pleasant immediately after, such as lunch with a friend to debrief or a cup of coffee."

You may also try drinking cold water or running cold water over your wrists, continues Ficken. " We may become hot and sweaty when we are anxious, and many of us hold our breath when we are anxious. Temperature fluctuations may control our body and respiration when we are anxious.

5. Be courteous to yourself

When you're aware that you're stuck in a loop of negative, anxious thoughts, it may be beneficial to converse with yourself as you would with a close friend or family member.

Instead of condemning or losing patience with yourself, try being kind and gently challenging yourself.

You could consider the last time you were this terrified and how things turned out better if you asked yourself, "Will worrying actually affect the outcome?"

Additionally, Gonzalez-Berrios suggests using affirmations to refocus your attention on a positive outlook.

When to require professional help

If you recognise that your anticipatory anxiety symptoms are becoming more chronic than situational and that your coping mechanisms are insufficient, it may be prudent to find a therapist and speak with them.

In addition to prescribing medication, a therapist may also employ cognitive behavioural therapy (CBT) techniques to help you manage your symptoms.

Ficken suggests contacting a therapist if one is available before the situation worsens.

In her words, "if you feel like you need assistance controlling your anxiety and tension and can't find a way out, you should seek assistance. It does not take long to master techniques for anxiety management, and they can be life-changing.

Let's recap

There is no official diagnosis of anticipatory anxiety. Instead, it falls under the category of generalised anxiety disorder.

It is normal to feel anxious and fearful about the future, and it is also normal to wish to avoid potentially dangerous or terrifying events. However, because you have no control over future events, it would be prudent to develop coping mechanisms for uncertainty.

Changing the focus of your attention and engaging in mindfulness exercises may help reduce feelings of anxiety. If possible, talking things over with a therapist may also help you manage your symptoms.

Chapter 4: Be Alert Regarding Your Thoughts

Be conscious of your thoughts and resist letting them consume you.

Without knowledge, one's thoughts can become overwhelming. Since it is written quite plainly in the Bible that man's heart is evil, learn it today.

There are so many errors we make in life; it is possible to have a conscious mind simply by having negative thoughts; identify what distracts and attracts you to negative thought. The majority of your actions reflect your inner thoughts.

Consider the questions below.

Are you optimistic or do you harbour doubts and pessimism?

Do you consider the positive aspects of a situation or the potential negative outcomes?

Do you think in terms of growth or stability?

Alexandra was the most knowledgeable museophile I've ever met; he knew what to expect in every museum in the state. Due to his devoted attention, he could provide a detailed history of every artefact discovered there, but he has never considered receiving a reward for his efforts.

His thoughts were pessimistic, and I was furious with him because he assists me whenever I want to write about history or culture. I could follow his advice to get the best work published, but he believed he was insufficient.

His mind was made up, and my attempts to convince him that he could organise a history webinar or programme, or perhaps write down his knowledge, were unsuccessful.

I decided to take him by surprise, obtained a recorder, and questioned him on history and culture. He felt insulted and wanted to demonstrate his intelligence to me.

I played him the recording of his confident speech, and he felt immensely proud of himself. Currently, he is a history and culture professor and TV host.

One self-assurance thought changed his entire life.

Despite what many believe, our thoughts are not set in stone. They are formed by recognising them and refusing to believe everything you think. The first conception of good, bad, and ugly thoughts occurs in the mind, and 80% of the probability of achieving one's goals, both successfully and unsuccessfully, is based on the mind.

There is a proverb that goes as follows: (what you believe in works for you).

I can say with pride that I am tried and true because there was a time when I was so consumed with negative thoughts that I imposed them on others.

Example: Whenever my friends share good news, I immediately ask, "What if you fail?" I evaluate my project as 50% negative and 50% positive, and it has dealt me poorly. Most of my plans failed miserably. Until I met Dr. James, I always saw the negative rather than the positive. He then told me that my thoughts can affect my entire life unconsciously, so if I can be so bold negatively, why shouldn't I devote all my energy to positivity and creating hope?

Simply dwelling on the negative strengthens its influence." The actress Shirley MacLaine.

Most of the time, when we consider becoming ill or anticipate sickness/death, it comes to pass.

Today, the majority of individuals are extremely health and body conscious. We take care of food selection and timing. When it comes to what we feed our minds, we have little concern.

The mind is very important, but many individuals are more concerned with the appearance of their skin than the content of their minds.

Unbeknownst to us, the mind remembers negative things more frequently than positive ones.

Perform the exercise below

Try remembering all of your childhood experiences and see what happens; the negative ones will always come back in full without any images or scars, but the positive ones will be difficult to recall.

Take a look around you. Whatever you are observing and listening to is mental nourishment. What you feed it today will determine your future.

This way of thinking influences our life decisions as well.

If your thoughts and intentions are pure, so will be your actions. If you feed your mind with negativity, it will eventually manifest in every action you perform.

There is too much negativity in the world today, so we must always be mindful of what to consume and what to avoid.

For instance, how often do you read or watch the news? Numerous individuals spend countless hours in front of the television, repeatedly viewing the same news. You are well aware of the proportion of positive to negative news there. The majority of them are negative. They may not affect you immediately, but they will eventually manifest in your thoughts and actions.

I'm not a fan of the news because it's filled with negative stories and messes with my head a lot, but I do listen to certain news stories to expand my understanding of history and culture. I always recommend that people have a reason for listening to the news.

To illustrate how it affects us in the long run, let us consider another illustration. What is the first thing that comes to mind when a loved one fails to return home on time? Do you fear that he or she has met with misfortune? There are numerous possibilities that he or she will be late, but your first thought would be "Oh, no!" There could be an accident or other unfortunate event."

Why do these types of negative thoughts dominate your mind at that time?

This is due to the fact that you have seen numerous news stories in which a person's tardiness was caused by a tragic event. Or you may have read similar tales in books. There is nothing inherently negative about reading and viewing such content, but moderation is required. Too much of it affects you profoundly and unintentionally.

Avoid negative people: avoid spending time with negative individuals. Yes, it is difficult to avoid those who are constantly in our vicinity. However, you must be cautious of those who consistently speak negatively.

They take pleasure in discussing the flaws of others because it allows them to temporarily conceal their own. Stop worrying about those who do not need your assistance. They're satisfied with themselves. Examine yourself and work on it instead.

Don't criticise others: We all enjoy gossiping about others. When some individuals complain about a celebrity, a politician, or even their neighbours, we inevitably join in. We even infiltrate their online personal lives and spew gibberish for hours. We are aware they will not listen to us and are unconcerned if they do. Stop criticising others and work on yourself instead.

Keep yourself occupied with something positive: If you only have an hour to go to your destination and you're sitting comfortably in a train, why not make the most of it? Read a book you've always wanted to read that will help you improve your skills or abilities.

For example, if you are driving, why don't you play some podcasts on your favourite subject? In this way, you are not only utilising that time to develop yourself, but also protecting your mind from the negativity around you. You will not experience anger while stuck in traffic because you will be preoccupied with something else.

Take a moment to pause, reflect, and then respond: No matter how much we filter the information entering our minds, we always pick up something negative here and there. And this is immediately reflected in our actions.

For instance, if someone is discussing something negative with us, we immediately lose control and begin doing the same. Remember that his actions are the result of his thoughts. However, it is not required to go with the flow.

It is always your choice how to react. One negative response will generate negative thought chains. Always pause, then think positively before responding. Always be positive in your thoughts and actions. (Deepak Rajpal)

"The mind is all there is. What do you anticipate becoming? – Buddha –

Imagine that everyone in your clique is discussing their rape experience, and you feel compelled to join in. This is not the case; you must not join the crowd, and not everyone must have a negative story to tell.

You can be different, negativity is contactable.

Chapter 5: Normal View And Magnified View.

A person with depression and anxiety disorder tends to magnify minor thoughts and generate a great deal of negative ones.

It is a normal occurrence for everyone. Every time we visit a crowded location, everyone has similar thoughts about themselves regarding the location and the surrounding environment. The only difference is that a person with social anxiety disorder magnifies these minor thoughts and begins to give them significance, whereas other people disregard these thoughts and do not give them importance. If you are able to decipher their gestures and body language, you will discover that such individuals who are accustomed to working and remaining in a crowd for extended periods of time spend countless hours surrounded by individuals who are highly stable. The first reason is that they become accustomed to living in a crowd, and the second is that they disregard trivial thoughts. Consider The Soldiers Who Protect Their Nation By Remaining On The Border Day And Night. Would it matter to them that people with social anxiety disorder frequently have trivial thoughts?

The more importance you give to minor negative thoughts, the more unstable your mind becomes and the more restlessness you experience. It is natural, in any social situation, for the situation to worsen the more we worry about damaging our own image. The same thoughts that a normal person sees through a normal perspective, a person suffering from social anxiety disorder sees through an enlarged perspective. This is why even the smallest, most trivial, and most negative thoughts can dominate your mind and cause you mental pain. You can easily overcome diseases such as depression and social anxiety disorder if you begin to give less importance to negative thoughts that arise in your mind and stop viewing them with a magnifying glass.

Chapter 6: Food Misconceptions: Have We Always Been Misled Regarding Healthy Eating?

Imagine your body as a collection of cells. Our microscopic cells make up 10% of what is alive in our physical body, while the remaining 90% consists of microorganisms residing in our gut, skin, and other tissues. 1 The food we consume has a profound effect on the microbiota in our gut. As previously discussed, the food we eat has the ability to either fortify and strengthen our intestinal barrier and gut microbiota or to gradually degrade them. Research continues to reveal the connection between the gut microbiome and common chronic diseases such as diabetes, heart disease, and Parkinson's disease; therefore, it is imperative that we learn how to take care of our gut and then do so. 2 Why are we still so confused about the nutrition our bodies require for nourishment and balance when we have more information than ever before about food and its interaction with the human body? Many of us have been told to eliminate dairy and gluten (and possibly other foods) without a detailed explanation as to why, so we simply assume they are unhealthy and lack a deeper understanding. Here are three possible causes for our confusion regarding healthy eating:

The marketing of food products by food companies disregards the impact on health.

Numerous experts and gurus promote specific food ideologies and diets as "the one" for all people, without placing sufficient emphasis on the bio-individuality of individuals. What is good for one person is poison for another.

We are largely ignorant of the fundamentals of nutrition and the fact that whole food nutrition is the basis for a healthy body and long life.

FOOD MARKETING

Food marketing influences us, and the manner in which it is conducted frequently leads us to believe things about food and its relationship to general health that are not necessarily true. Since the 1950s, food processing has helped the economy become more profitable, but it has not had the same positive effects on our health. The media then writes a headline that has a profound effect on our understanding of the benefit and manipulates us into believing that consuming this food will reduce the risk of heart disease. As an illustration, the macadamia nut company Royal Hawaiian Nuts petitioned the FDA to be able to use the following statement on their food packaging: "Supportive but inconclusive evidence suggests that eating 1.5 oz of macadamia nuts daily as part of a diet low in saturated fat and cholesterol and not resulting in an increase in saturated fat or calories may reduce the risk of coronary heart disease." In response, the FDA issued a statement in 2017 and began requiring more disclaimers on product packaging. They desired to avoid liability if someone felt that the health information on these packages was misleading. In addition to selective advertising, the companies that produce these foods also fund research into the health benefits of consuming them. Royal Hawaiian Macadamia Nuts' petition to the FDA included a Hershey's-funded research study on macadamia nuts covered in chocolate. Sellers marketing their food are aware that a health statement from the FDA has the ability to effectively spread their message to the masses and that people will trust such a statement.

Being healthy and preventing disease depends less on whether you consume a specific food for the health benefits it provides and more on the totality of the foods you consume. The point is that it is not a single food that reduces the risk of heart disease and cancer, but rather a combination of foods, lifestyle, environment, and genetics that influence health outcomes.

Chapter 7: The Range Of Professional Recommendations

Why do so many experts recommend radically dissimilar diets? This will baffle you until you realise how bio-individuality and personalised nutrition can make or break an individual's health. It is not the case that there is only one truth and multiple experts are mistaken. One of the keys to healing your gut and optimising your health is recognising the bio-individuality philosophy, which asserts that each individual has unique needs. It supports the notion that while a particular food or diet may be suitable for one person, it may cause inflammation in another. 5 Consequently, while one individual may benefit from a plant-based diet, another individual may benefit from a ketogenic diet. How can this be when their diets are so dissimilar? This exemplifies the marvel of bio-individuality in action.

WHOLE DIETARY NUTRITION

In addition to the never-ending diet theories we must decipher, it is important to note that what was recommended as a balanced diet thirty years ago differs significantly from what is recommended today. The Food Pyramid Guide was published by the

United States government in 1992 to demonstrate to Americans what constituted a healthy diet. Today's rates of obesity, diabetes, heart disease, hormone imbalances, digestive disorders, and insulin resistance indicate that the 1992 recommendation that the majority of our diet consist of bread, pasta, and grains was incorrect.

Chapter 8: Complex PTSD Manifestations

These conditions contribute to a variety of anxiety, addiction, eating disorders, and depression. When one disorder is present, the likelihood of having a second or third disorder is significantly increased. The psychological effects of this condition will continue to amplify and may cause irreparable damage to your life. Although assistance is always available, it is not always simple to ask for it, especially if you are embarrassed or have trouble admitting that something is wrong.

The problem with avoidance is that it neither eliminates nor ameliorates the condition. In actuality, ignoring a problem, particularly one of a psychological or emotional nature, only makes matters worse. By avoiding a thorough examination of the issues, you are lighting the fuse for an explosion. This explosion, while symbolic, can lead to a variety of self-harming behaviours, such as adultery, theft, abusive behaviour, tantrums, and manipulation, which may not be a part of who you truly are. Instead, they are the result of trauma that has been repressed due to discomfort or awkwardness.

Become Accustomed to Being Uncomfortable

One of the initial steps in this workbook is determining how to adhere to your recovery plan, even when things become difficult or uncomfortable - because they will. On occasion, you will feel so uneasy that you want to crawl out of your skin.

However, you can take a deep breath and reassure your discomfort that everything will be alright. The discomfort will pass quickly.

And you can become accustomed to being uncomfortable.

This may sound like an oxymoron, but it is an essential component of recovery.

Without putting yourself in uncomfortable situations (not risky situations; there is a significant distinction), you cannot grow.

If you do not grow, you will spend your entire life like a hamster on a wheel. You will always be looking forward, struggling to keep up, but never advancing. You may receive a promotion at work but still feel dissatisfied. There will always be a shadow over your shoulder, a dark veil over your heart, and unrelenting tension within your body.

You may awaken in the middle of the night and dwell on the same thought — something that occurred five, ten, or fifteen years ago, or even longer. These thoughts can keep you up at night and convince you that you are a bad person, that everything you do is wrong, or something equally damning.

None of these are beneficial. None will provide you with the self-love and care you deserve.

Instead, make a plan to become accustomed to discomfort.

Perhaps this will appear differently to each individual. You must determine what works best for you. However, the following are some helpful tips, suggestions, and ways to find solace.

Take Notice Of Your Pain

This unease can occur in a movie theatre, grocery store, football game, conversation, or at home.

Instead of avoiding the discomfort and quickly pushing it away, investigate its source. Are you in a dimly lit area? Are you discussing a specific topic? Do you observe something that is upsetting? Are there too many individuals nearby? Are there not enough individuals present?

Determine the cause of your discomfort by conducting an investigation.

There is a good chance that you will experience considerable discomfort in many locations. However, that's okay. If you feel overwhelmed by the amount of discomfort you are experiencing, remove yourself from the situation to remind yourself that you do have control. Although they may feel strange, your emotions need not dictate your thoughts and actions.

This type of self-reflection will require some effort, so don't be too hard on yourself if your emotions take over initially (or even after practicing). There are always times when we are vulnerable, and it is typically during these times that the feeling of discomfort hits hardest, knocking you back on your heels.

Instruments useful for this method:

PEN, PENCIL, JOURNAL, OR LAPTOP. Journaling enables you to see your thoughts. In addition, it helps clear the mind. These two components are essential to self-reflection and extremely useful when determining what makes you uneasy. It is likely that you will develop the daily journaling habit; this is a beneficial practise. It will provide you with unique insight into yourself that you may not have had before. When keeping a journal, write your thoughts freely and without judgement, even if they are negative. Then, when you are finished writing, you can see that perhaps what you are thinking and how you are feeling aren't connected, because your thoughts aren't as bad as they appear to be when they are trapped inside your head.

PRACTICE MINDFULNESS. Mindfulness is a keyword that has been overused and can have multiple meanings. However, it will be one of your most useful tools. Mindfulness is defined as complete awareness of something. Nevertheless, for psychological reasons, you will focus exclusively on the present state. During mindfulness practise, you observe and experience your emotions, thoughts, and bodily sensations without judgment[5]. This statement indicates that you will not avoid unpleasant situations. You will simply be.

YOGA—

Yoga may not be for everyone, but if you have C-PTSD, it will help calm your mind. Then, you pay attention to your body. Consider it an additional mindfulness exercise. Don't worry if you've never done yoga before. There are numerous online, print, studio, and gym resources for beginners. You need not be particularly flexible, perform headstands, or become a vegan. Simply be present in your body while concentrating on a routine. If you are unable to perform the poses to their fullest extent, that is acceptable; it will give you something to strive for. However, yoga is a place to release and reflect on the emotions you are experiencing in the present.

Grab a pillow, chair, couch, or bed, or whatever else you need to be comfortable for five to ten minutes of daily meditation. You may sit or lie down; this will not be an intense meditation practise. You sit with your eyes closed and hands relaxed as you listen to your thoughts. That is the conclusion. Simply, you will have the opportunity to connect with your emotions, mind, and body.

- BE INFORMED ON C-PTSD AND MINDFULNESS. There are numerous online and printed resources available for research. If you have sought out a therapist and believe they are a good fit for you, then you should request some helpful resources from them. The greater your knowledge, the greater your comprehension of your reactions, emotions, and other responses to specific situations.

You are not required to use all of the tools listed above immediately or for the rest of your life. Incorporating a multitude of activities into your daily routine will not accelerate your understanding of your disorder. It is likely that you will hyper-focus on helpful tools for a few weeks, and then lose interest in them as you become exhausted from adopting new practises.

Instead, proceed slowly. It is not a battle to be fought; rather, it is a complex puzzle whose pieces have not yet been revealed. You will uncover them layer by layer, and each time you unravel one and become accustomed to the process, another layer will surface and require your attention.

When you decide to manage your recovery, you assist yourself in the most beneficial way possible. There will be times of greatness and times of failure. There will be times when the C-PTSD will have you so mired in despair that it will seem impossible to escape. However, you will always prevail. Even when it's difficult, and especially when it's unpleasant, you must persevere and keep going.

In this section, you will learn the difference between PTSD and C-PTSD, gain a deeper understanding of C-PTSD symptoms, and see how C-PTSD affects your daily and future life, as well as your relationships with others.

Skills and Strategies for Coping with Anxiety and Stress

Developing a repertoire of coping strategies and skills is a crucial step in managing anxiety and stress. These are techniques for managing your emotions, thoughts, and behaviours in response to stressful or anxious situations. By having a variety of coping skills and strategies available to you, you will be better equipped to handle challenges and maintain your mental health and wellbeing.

There are a variety of effective coping skills and strategies for managing anxiety and stress. Common examples include:

Cognitive-behavioral therapy (CBT) focuses on modifying negative thought patterns and behaviours that contribute to anxiety and stress. You will learn how to identify and challenge negative thoughts and replace them with more realistic and positive ones through cognitive behavioural therapy. You will also learn skills and techniques to manage anxiety and stress in the present, such as deep breathing, progressive muscle relaxation, and exposure therapy (facing your fears gradually).

Exposure therapy is a form of therapy that helps you gradually confront your fears in a safe and controlled environment. This can aid in the management of anxiety and stress associated with specific phobias and other anxiety disorders. By gradually exposing yourself to your fears, you can learn to more effectively manage your anxiety and stress.

Relaxation techniques, such as deep breathing, progressive muscle relaxation, and meditation, can reduce the physical manifestations of anxiety and stress, including racing thoughts, rapid breathing, and muscle tension. These techniques can also improve your overall mood and sense of well-being by fostering a sense of relaxation and calm.

Regular physical activity can reduce anxiety and stress by stimulating the release of endorphins, which promote feelings of happiness and well-being. Physical symptoms of anxiety and stress, such as rapid breathing and muscle tension, can also be alleviated through exercise.

In order to effectively manage anxiety and stress, it is essential to practice good sleep hygiene. Establishing good sleep hygiene practises, such as adhering to a consistent sleep schedule, creating a relaxing bedtime routine, and avoiding screens before bedtime, can help improve sleep quality.

Mindfulness is the practice of focusing one's attention on the present moment without judgement. This can help you become more conscious of your thoughts and emotions and enable you to respond to them with greater equilibrium. Meditation and yoga can reduce anxiety and stress by fostering a sense of calm and relaxation.

Sometimes, finding a way to temporarily distract yourself from anxious or stressful thoughts can be beneficial.

Engaging in enjoyable activities, such as hobbies, spending time with family and friends, or reading a book, can help you forget your worries.

Self-care: Taking care of your physical and emotional needs is an essential component of anxiety and stress management. Self-care activities, such as getting enough sleep, eating a healthy diet, and engaging in enjoyable activities, can improve your overall health and stress resistance.

Chapter 9: Taking Control Of Stress And Anxiety

Both mental and physical health are severely compromised by stress and anxiety. Both are common reactions and emotions that can spiral out of control and necessitate professional assistance.

In this chapter, we will identify the distinctions between the two, as well as the causes of problematic stress and worry that are distinct from everyday anxiety, and what you can do to obtain relief.

An overview of anxiety and tension

Stress and anxiety are everyday emotions and behaviours for some individuals. We all experience this at various times and to varying degrees. Both can be overwhelming and disrupt your life, but there are substantial differences between the two. The most significant fact is that anxiety disorders can be categorized as a particular type of mental illness. Whether you struggle with stress, anxiety, or both, it is essential that you understand how to treat it. You can control your responses and emotions with the aid of treatment, which will reduce your levels of stress and anxiety.

Chapter 10: What Is Stress?

Any physical or mental demand is a source of stress. It may be caused by any circumstance or event that frustrates or stresses you. Stress is a completely normal response of the body to a change, threat, or pressure. Physical, mental, and emotional responses are all possible. Everyone experiences periods of stress throughout their lives. Some individuals may react to stimuli more strongly or frequently than others.

Stress can be both beneficial and detrimental. When you are under constructive stress, you are motivated to complete tasks, do them correctly, and concentrate on activities.

Chronic and overwhelming stress, however, is detrimental to mental and physical health. Stress can cause heart disease, depression, physical discomfort, insomnia, digestive issues, loneliness, dietary and weight changes, and even heart disease.

Anxiety is characterised by fear, concern, or unease. It may occur due to stress, but it can also occur for no apparent reason. For instance, you may experience test-related anxiety out of concern that you will perform poorly. Anxiety is frequently induced by stressful circumstances or situations, and vice versa.

When anxiety spirals out of control and has a significant negative impact on your life, it becomes a problem. Both chronic stress and excessive anxiety can cause both emotional and physical suffering. High anxiety or an anxiety disorder can prevent you from engaging in activities such as catching up with friends, going to work or school, or trying something new.

Chapter 11: The Distinction Between Anxiety And Tension

Anxiety and stress have separate origins.

Frequently, situations induce stress. Once the issue has been resolved, you will no longer feel anxious.

Perhaps you are worried about an upcoming test, or you are caring for three young children while working from home. In both instances, there is a stressor. After the exam or when your children return to daycare, your anxiety decreases. Nonetheless, stress is not always transient. Chronic stress is a pervasive form of stress caused by a demanding occupation or family problem.

In contrast, anxiety can occur without an obvious stressor. Due to their overlap, stress and anxiety are frequently used interchangeably. Anxiety and stress both activate the fight-or-flight response and have similar physical effects. However, anxiety is not always obvious. Anxiety focuses on our worries or fears regarding potential threats, in addition to our discomfort with the anxiety itself.

Stress and anxiety are normal human emotions, but they can become problematic if they last too long or negatively impact our health or way of life.

Despite the fact that stress and anxiety are two distinct concepts, they are interconnected.

Stress can sometimes be the cause of anxiety. For instance, if you're anxious about an impending major relocation, you may notice that you're anxious about everything.

Chapter 12: Trying To Act Happy

You Are Not Alone in Pretending to Be Happy You are not alone when it comes to making an effort to be joyful. It occurs sufficiently frequently. Many of us have pretended to be happy at some point, and this may occur more frequently than we realise. Perhaps we're having a terrible day, but we don't want to make our loved ones feel bad, so we put on a happy face and act as if everything is fine. In the near future, it may be normal for us to occasionally feel down but not to wish to make others feel down. Putting on a pleasant front for others is not always immoral; in fact, it demonstrates moral concern for their well-being. However, if you find yourself pretending more and more, you may discover that this can become a destructive or incapacitating habit.

The Problem of Pretending to Be Happy

Consider the most recent time you faked happiness. Did it make a significant difference? Certainly, someone else must have felt great, but how do you feel? If anything, acting made you feel worse than you normally would have. When you pretend everything is fine when you are truly miserable, it is unlikely that you are helping anyone.

Recognize that the person you're attempting to persuade does not require your assistance because they care about your happiness above all else. You might be able to persuade them a few times, but they will eventually realise that you're only pretending to be pleased. When this occurs, the individual may feel worse for not noticing it sooner. They may believe that they have let you down and are not following your instructions.

Despite the fact that you could fake happiness out of concern for others, doing so is likely to deplete your energy even further. This may lead to more complicated negative emotions. On some level, you are perplexed as to why your loved ones do not assist you and cannot see through your façade. On a deeper level, you wish you didn't have to fake at all or that others would see through your facade. Probably, you are tired of maintaining this facade and wish you could simply be yourself, regardless of how that may appear.

Appearing happy can be detrimental to both your relationships and your mental health. It may appear that acting joyfully would improve your relationships and the dispositions of those around you, but this is not the case. You are concealing your true emotions and experiences from them, which will affect how you feel and interact with the people in your life.

What Have You Got to Hide?

When they are experiencing the symptoms of mental health issues such as anxiety and depression, many people attempt to appear cheerful. Depression is a serious but treatable mental health issue that can be cured with the aid of qualified professionals. It is essential to communicate with those closest to you in a straightforward and honest manner. Informing those closest to you and most important to you could be advantageous. Whether it be your spouse, close friends, or parents, you must have people in your corner to help you through difficult times in your life.

When you are able to open up to someone and fully express yourself, you will have the chance to process your emotions in a genuine way. In the end, it is difficult to overcome what you refuse to acknowledge. You will not be able to overcome it if you do not acknowledge to anyone other than yourself that you are feeling stuck, upset, angry, or any other emotion. Disorders of the mind do not permit such freedom. They frequently cling to you and may make it appear impossible for you to continue with your life.

Hiding your negative emotions and thoughts will only cause you to disregard and disregard them. They frequently decline from there. Consider it comparable to the meals you prepare at home. You may glance at them and decide you don't want to deal with it at the moment, in which case you ignore them. If you continue to do this daily, you will quickly exhaust your options and be forced to deal with the mounting pile of dishes. The suppressed emotions function in a similar manner. They will intensify the longer you disregard them and refuse to confront them.

Accepting Your Feelings

The most important action you can take is to express your emotions openly. The initial step is a simple exchange of information. Working through whatever you're experiencing and initiating the process of regaining a sense of normalcy for yourself could be time-consuming and difficult. However, it is feasible, and there are techniques and resources available to assist you. The initial step is to always be honest and open.

To discuss what you've been suppressing for so long and what you're truly going through, you may need to put yourself in a very vulnerable position. But you'll likely be glad you did when you can express yourself authentically and feel heard and understood. You could feel a weight lift off your shoulders simply because the problem is being discussed openly.

The next step is ensuring that you obtain the necessary assistance. You do not need to face this challenge alone. You may not be able to obtain all the necessary resources from your loved ones and dependable individuals. A qualified, certified, and seasoned mental health professional can help you get started on your journey. Although the love and support of family and friends can inspire, motivate, and encourage you, only a qualified therapist or psychiatrist can provide you with the knowledge you need to move forward.

Obtaining Skilled Assistance

BetterHelp is an online service that connects individuals in need of therapy with licenced therapists. This program is entirely online, and it can provide you with the helpful information and invaluable assistance you need to move forward. According to scientific research, online counselling is effective in assisting people with a variety of difficulties, including depression, anxiety, feelings of sadness and unfulfillment, and more. In 2018, a study was conducted to determine the effect of online cognitive behavioural pain treatment on the reduction of disability, anxiety, and depression. After eight weeks of coursework, the authors of the study found that 76% of participants completed the course with an average grade of 85%, a 36% reduction in depressive symptoms, and a 32% reduction in anxiety symptoms.

Online counselling is convenient and cost-effective. No longer is it necessary to physically visit an office to schedule an appointment. You will not have to worry about being observed as you enter a clinic or other location. Instead, you will be able to consult with a therapist from the comfort of your own home. Because only an Internet connection is required, there are no restrictions on where sessions may be held. In addition, you will have the option to choose a candidate who resides everywhere, not just in your hometown.

Falsifying the appearance of happiness does not make a person evil. It is natural to desire the happiness of those around us. But you do not need to conceal your true emotions, especially if you are depressed, anxious, lonely, or lost. Individuals experience happiness differently; therefore, it may be beneficial to consult a trained therapist in order to determine how to comprehend and pursue it most efficiently.

Chapter 13: Emotional Mastery In Interpersonal Relationships: Enhancing Communication And Bonding

Emotional mastery is the ability to comprehend, regulate, and express one's emotions in oneself and in interactions with others. It is a significant component of emotional intelligence and crucial for establishing and maintaining healthy, meaningful relationships.

In partnerships, effective communication is a crucial component of emotional mastery. When we can express our emotions effectively and clearly, we are better able to connect with others, resolve conflicts, and build rapport. However, communicating emotions can be challenging because they are typically complex and difficult to articulate.

Active listening is a technique for improving communication and connection in relationships. This requires paying attention to what the other person is saying, including not only hearing their words but also attempting to comprehend their perspective and emotions.

When we listen attentively, we demonstrate to the other person our genuine interest in what they have to say and our concern for their feelings. Additionally, we may use open-ended questions to encourage the other person to reveal more about themselves and their emotions.

The ability to regulate our own emotions is a crucial element of emotional mastery in relationships.

When we are able to control our emotions, we are better equipped to deal with disagreements and difficult situations in a healthy and productive manner.

This can be achieved by taking deep breaths, counting to ten, or engaging in activities that help us relax and calm down. Having a network of friends and family who can provide emotional support when we are suffering is also beneficial.

In addition to being able to control our own emotions, it is equally important to be able to recognise and comprehend those of others. This requires paying close attention to nonverbal cues such as facial expressions, body language, and voice tone.

When we correctly interpret these signs, we are better equipped to respond to the needs and emotions of others in a helpful and compassionate manner.

Empathy is another method for improving communication and connection in relationships.

This involves attempting to understand the other person's thoughts and experiences by adopting their point of view. When we are able to put ourselves in the other person's shoes and demonstrate that we care about their feelings, we may be able to build trust and intimacy in the relationship.

It is also essential that we are able to express our emotions in a healthy and productive manner. This may involve discussing our emotions with the other individual or seeking the assistance of a therapist or counsellor.

When we are able to express our emotions in a healthy way, we can build stronger relationships with others and resolve issues more effectively.

In conclusion, emotional mastery is a crucial component of successful and rewarding relationships. By practising active listening, controlling our own emotions, recognising and comprehending the emotions of others, exercising empathy, and expressing our own emotions in a healthy manner, we can improve communication and connection in our relationships.

Chapter 14: Causes Of Bipolar Disorder And Anxiety Disorders

Bipolar disorder and anxiety disorders are two extremely complex and frequently misunderstood mental health conditions that affect millions of people worldwide. While they may appear unrelated, research has revealed that a variety of underlying causes contribute to the occurrence of both diseases.

Heredity is one of the primary causes of bipolar disorder. According to studies, those with a family history of bipolar disorder are significantly more likely to develop the disorder. Up to 85 percent of patients with bipolar disorder have a relative with the disorder. This indicates that there is a substantial genetic component to the development of bipolar disorder, although it is not entirely clear how this occurs.

Environmental factors may also contribute to the onset of bipolar disorder. Mania or depression can be triggered by stressful or traumatic events, such as the loss of a loved one or a major life change. Substance abuse, specifically drug or alcohol abuse, has also been linked to the development of bipolar disorder.

It is also known that anxiety disorders have both genetic and environmental causes. Those with a family history of anxiety disorders are more likely to develop the disease, as is the case with bipolar disorder. The emergence of anxiety disorders may be influenced by stress, trauma, and substance abuse.

Physiological issues, such as an overactive thyroid or low blood sugar, and certain drugs, such as stimulants or antidepressants, are additional causes of anxiety disorders. Some individuals may also develop anxiety disorders as a result of adverse life circumstances, such as abuse, neglect, or major life transitions.

Despite the fact that these factors may contribute to the development of bipolar disorder and anxiety disorders, they are not the only ones at play. Several genetic, environmental, and other factors likely contribute to the development of these disorders, which are extraordinarily complex.

Despite the complexity of these conditions, there is hope for those who suffer from bipolar disorder and anxiety disorders. With the right treatment, such as counselling, medication, and changes in lifestyle, individuals can learn to manage their symptoms and lead fulfilling, purposeful lives. If you or someone you know is battling bipolar disorder or an anxiety disorder, it is essential to seek the assistance of a trained mental health professional. Together, you may attempt to determine the causes of these diseases and devise a plan for effectively managing them.

Genetics

The Role of Genes in Causing Bipolar and Anxiety Disorders

Bipolar disorder and anxiety disorders are two mental health conditions that can have a significant impact on an individual's quality of life. These conditions are characterised by significant mood swings, difficulty managing emotions, and difficulties with day-to-day functioning. Although the precise aetiology of many problems is unknown, there is evidence that genetics play a role in their development.

According to one study, individuals with a family history of bipolar disorder are four to six times more likely to develop the disorder. Likewise, individuals with a family history of anxiety disorders are more likely to develop these issues. This indicates that there is a genetic component to the development of these diseases.

In numerous ways, genetics may influence the development of these disorders. For instance, genetic variations may increase a person's risk of developing bipolar disorder or anxiety disorders. Changes in the way the brain processes and regulates emotions may contribute to the development of these diseases.

Genetics may also influence the severity of certain diseases. Due to hereditary factors, some people may have more severe bipolar disorder or anxiety disorder symptoms, while others may have fewer symptoms. This may make it difficult to predict how a patient will respond to treatment and how effectively they will manage their symptoms.

Despite the fact that genetics plays a significant role in the development of bipolar and anxiety disorders, it is essential to note that these issues are not entirely predetermined by genetics. Stress, trauma, and life events may also contribute to the development of these illnesses.

Although it is impossible to avoid developing bipolar illness or anxiety disorders, understanding the role of genetics in their development may help individuals better manage their symptoms and seek treatment. This may result in improved outcomes and a higher quality of life for those affected by these diseases.

Environmental Factors

Environmental factors have a significant influence on the onset and progression of bipolar and anxiety disorders. Multiple factors, including genetics, brain chemistry, and life experiences, typically contribute to the complexity of these conditions. However, research indicates that environmental factors may significantly increase the likelihood of contracting these diseases.

Stress is an environmental factor that has been linked to the development of bipolar disorder. Stressful life events, such as the death of a loved one, financial difficulties, or a major life transition, may precipitate the onset of bipolar disorder. Additionally, stress may exacerbate the symptoms of bipolar disorder, causing more severe and frequent mood swings.

Social interaction quality is another environmental factor that may contribute to the development of bipolar and anxiety disorders. It has been demonstrated that individuals with strong social support networks have lower rates of anxiety and depression. On the other hand, stressed or socially isolated individuals may be more susceptible to these illnesses.

Additionally, living in a dangerous or unhealthy environment may contribute to the development of bipolar and anxiety disorders. Pollution, hazardous chemicals, and other hazardous substances may severely impair brain function and increase the risk of mental health problems.

In addition, traumatic events, such as physical, sexual, or psychological abuse, may increase the likelihood of developing anxiety and bipolar disorders. These occurrences may cause severe mental anguish and contribute to the development of mental disorders.

The frequency and presentation of bipolar and anxiety disorders may also be affected by sociocultural and cultural factors. For instance, cultural expectations and social norms may contribute to the stigmatisation of mental health disorders, resulting in inadequate support and treatment. In addition, certain cultures may have higher rates of stress and social isolation, which may increase the likelihood of contracting these diseases.

Environmental factors have a significant impact on the development and progression of bipolar and anxiety disorders. It is essential to address these factors in order to provide appropriate support and treatment for individuals with these disorders. By fostering a welcoming and wholesome environment, we can reduce the incidence of bipolar and anxiety disorders and improve the lives of those affected by these conditions.

Chapter 15: How To You Stress Free

Physical and psychological stress is a common response to the demands and difficulties of daily life. It is a normal aspect of life that may motivate you to meet deadlines, prepare for tests, and exert your best effort. On the other hand, persistent or poorly managed stress can be detrimental to both your physical and mental health.

There are numerous distinct causes of stress, including those related to work, relationships, finances, and daily responsibilities. Stress can manifest in numerous ways, including anxiety, irritability, difficulty sleeping, and physical symptoms such as headaches, stomachaches, and tense muscles.

Identifying the causes of stress in your life is a prerequisite for finding healthy solutions for managing stress. This may consist of techniques such as meditation, physical activity, and time management. It is essential to strike a balance between your daily obligations and your physical and emotional needs.

We can recognise stress when it overwhelms us or causes problems.

On other days, we accept it, content to live in a world where new pressures arise as old ones subside. Typically, we locate our stress externally, in our surroundings and the stress's apparent causes. According to national studies, the leading sources of stress are money, employment, health issues, the health of our families, international news, and children. These studies also demonstrate a correlation between the stress levels of Americans and their propensity for unhealthy behaviours such as comfort eating, smoking, inactivity, and sedentary behaviour.

However, how well do you comprehend and manage your stress? Have you ever noticed that a situation that causes you minimal stress one day can be extremely stressful the next? Therapists and other healthcare professionals are aware that stress builds up and that our ability to cope with it depends on numerous variables that vary from day to day and even hour to hour. Important are improved self-care and general physical and mental health. People with greater social support typically respond to and recover from stress more effectively. In order to detect early signs of stress-related issues, it is also advisable to have regular physicals.

It is essential to recognise that everyone experiences situations in which they feel overburdened and overworked.

According to psychologists, "crises" occur when a person's ability to cope with a stressful situation is exceeded. During these difficult times, it is imperative to seek assistance from family, friends, the community, and perhaps a professional. The majority of people can demonstrate resilience, recover from setbacks, gain insight from them, and continue living their lives if they are handled properly. When mishandled, a temporary crisis can become an ongoing problem.

Understanding stress will help you better manage it. However, understanding your stress response is crucial. What stresses you out? What worries you the most? Your body (tension, respiration, heart rate), thoughts (worrying), emotions (anger and irritation, melancholy), and behaviour (isolation, negative behaviours) are all examples of how your stress response "appears."

If you are not aware of your stress until it manifests in problems in these areas, it may be time to "tune in" to what your body and mind are trying to tell you. It may also be time for you to acquire more efficient stress management techniques.

STRESS-MIND-BODY CONNECTION

Have you ever wondered why, when under stress and depression, you suddenly feel so exhausted and your muscles ache all over your body? This is because your mind and body respond simultaneously to your emotions.

The connection between our physical and mental selves is intricate. Since their inception, medicine and science have been aware of the body's influence on the mind. In a reflective manner, their connection controls emotions, diseases, and physical health.

On the other hand, these emotions trigger a cascade of physiological changes that affect blood chemistry, cell and organ function, and heart rate.

Thoughts that are stressful cause the release of stress hormones, which impede the body's ability to recover. Under stress, the stress hormones tend to suppress immunological responses. The stress hormone that people are most familiar with is adrenaline.

These chemicals cause your body to respond to stressful situations by placing you in an arousal state, which causes your heart to beat faster, your blood pressure to rise, your muscles to contract, your metabolism to speed up, and an adrenaline rush.

The body will either adapt to stress or respond to it. When your mind or body is asked to do something, you comply. This reaction is referred to as the flight-or-fight response. In addition, this is the body's involuntary response to a threat or danger. When a threat is present, the body releases hormones that quicken the heart rate and release stored energy, preparing the subject for flight or combat.

The survival response is triggered by stress. Stress prevents you from fleeing or fighting, but adrenaline still enters your bloodstream. This may result in heart attacks, anxiety, high blood pressure, insomnia, an irregular heartbeat, depression, and aggression.

EFFECT OF STRESS ON WOMEN

Women are experiencing greater levels of stress than ever before. As they attempt to juggle family and professional responsibilities, they are under tremendous strain. They frequently put their own needs last while juggling the needs of others and maintaining a delicate balance.

The body releases powerful hormones such as adrenaline, cortisol, and oxytocin in response to stress. The "fight or flight" response is triggered by adrenaline, which prepares the body for a quick response. The body responds to stress by increasing its respiration, heart rate, and blood pressure. When excessive quantities of adrenaline are secreted, the body may react by experiencing vertigo or heart palpitations.

Cortisol, the primary stress hormone, is known to increase blood pressure and blood sugar levels, reduce immune system function, and inhibit growth, digestion, and the reproductive and reproductive systems. An apple-shaped physique and fat accumulation around the waist and hips are the results of excessive cortisol production.

Oxytocin stimulates both lactation-induced milk production and uterine contractions during labour. Moreover, it is believed to strengthen the emotional bond between mother and child. The body overcompensates for chronic stress by releasing a steady stream of stress chemicals. Overproduction of stress hormones may contribute to obesity, insomnia, heart disease, depression, digestive issues, and other disorders. According to scientific studies, the overproduction of stress hormones may inhibit the release of stomach acid and stimulate the colon. Constipation, diarrhoea, and irritable bowel syndrome are frequent gastrointestinal complaints among women who experience chronic stress.

Overproduction of stress hormones may weaken the immune system and increase the risk of contracting infections. It may cause excessive cytokine production, resulting in excessive inflammation. Women with autoimmune diseases such as Lupus, Multiple Sclerosis, or Rheumatoid Arthritis may find this extremely unpleasant. Asthma attacks and lupus flare-ups can be triggered by stress. Cortisol's byproducts have sedative properties and may cause depression. Symptoms of stress-induced depression include sleep disturbances, weight loss, and diminished libido. Additionally, it may result in personality or behavioral issues.

Due to prolonged exposure to an overproduction of stress hormones, your heart rate, blood pressure, and cholesterol levels may all increase. These variables may make you more susceptible to heart disease and stroke. Although stress is a normal part of life, you can control its impact. Hypnosis and meditation are both extremely effective stress-reduction techniques. To practice meditation, you need only sit still, relax your muscles, and focus on your breathing. After less than 15 minutes of meditation, you may experience relaxation and renewal.

It has been demonstrated that hypnosis induces the body's natural relaxation response. It may help you modify your stress response and promotes your mental and physical health. Consider incorporating meditation or hypnosis into your daily routine if you suffer from chronic stress. Obtain assistance from a Certified Hypnotherapist if you have never utilized these techniques before. A few sessions are required before you can practice these stress-relieving techniques on your own.

EFFECT OF STRESS ON MEN

Males and females may react differently to stress. According to some studies, stressed men may be more likely to engage in risky behaviors such as smoking and overeating. Men may also be less likely to seek help or voice their concerns. As a result, men may find it more difficult to manage stress, which may have negative effects on their mental and physical health.

Males' physical and psychological health may be significantly impacted by stress.

Chapter 16: Anxiety Disorder

Anxiety disorder is a mental health condition characterized by persistent and excessive worry about a variety of situations or activities.

People with anxiety disorders frequently exhibit physical symptoms such as an elevated heart rate, profuse sweating, trembling, and breathing difficulties. These symptoms may lead to avoidance of certain situations or activities and may interfere with daily activities.

Anxiety disorders include generalized anxiety disorder, panic disorder, social anxiety disorder, and specific phobias.

Generalized anxiety disorder is characterised by persistent and excessive anxiety regarding a variety of situations, including work, school, and relationships. These anxieties can interfere with daily activities and result in physical symptoms such as muscle tension, fatigue, and trouble sleeping.

Panic disorder is characterized by recurrent, unexpected panic attacks, which can include physical symptoms such as heart palpitations, shortness of breath, and chest pain.

Various situations or activities can trigger panic attacks, which may lead to avoidance of those situations or activities.

Social anxiety disorder is characterized by an extreme dread of social or performance situations, such as public speaking or interacting with others.

This fear may manifest physically as flushing, perspiration, and difficulty speaking.

Specific phobias are extreme fears of particular situations or objects, such as heights, animals, or blood. These phobias may result in avoidance of the feared objects or situations and may hinder daily activities.

Anxiety disorders are treatable through a combination of psychotherapy, medication, and self-care techniques. Cognitive-behavioral therapy can assist individuals with anxiety disorders in identifying and altering negative thought patterns and behaviors that contribute to their anxiety. Medication, such as selective serotonin reuptake inhibitors (SSRIs) and benzodiazepines, can assist in alleviating anxiety symptoms.

Techniques of self-care, such as relaxation techniques and exercise, can also be useful in the management of anxiety. Anxiety disorders should be treated because they can interfere with daily life and lead to other issues, such as depression.

www.ingramcontent.com/pod-product-compliance
Lightning Source LLC
Chambersburg PA
CBHW050232120526
44590CB00016B/2061